Made in the USA
Coppell, TX
10 May 2023

16686994R10072